Author Information

Blockchain, Bitcoin and Altcoins: A comprehensive Guide

Series 1

1st October 2020

Website: https://avilandigitalsolutions.com

Written by Bonface Juma

Declaration

This book is for educational and general information purposes only. It is not advice or recommendation for investment decisions.

The author and the publisher are not liable to any loses occurring due to negligence or otherwise, resulting from the use of this book or reliance on information provided in this book.

Table of Contents

LIST OF TABLES

LIST OF FIGURES

LIST OF GRAPHS

ABBREVIATIONS AND ACRONYMS

ASIC	Application-specific integrated circuit
ATM	Automated Teller Machine
BCH	Bitcoin Cash
BTC	Bitcoin
DNS	Domain Name System
ERC-20	Ethereum token used for smart contracts
ETH	Ethereum
HODL hold)	Hold (used in cryptocurrency arena to mean
HYIP	High Yielding Investment Plan
IOT	Internet of Things
KYC	Know Your Client
OTP	One-time password (passcode)
Pos	Proof of stake
Pow	Proof of work
Scrypt	Password based key derivation function
SEPA	Single Euro Payments Area
SHA-256	Secure Hash Algorithm-256
SPDI	Special Purpose Depository Institution
USD	United States Dollar
X11	Windowing system for bitmap displays
XRP	Ripple

CHAPTER ONE

MEANING OF CRYPTOCURRENCY

A cryptocurrency (or a virtual currency) is a digital asset based on computer network deigned to work as a medium of exchange. It can be used as a form of online payment for goods and services. It can also be used to pay bills, do shopping or be held as a financial asset and then sold off for profit.

Cryptocurrencies do not exist in tangible forms such as paper money rather they exist in form of computer transactions which are stored in a computerized ledger secured by cryptography. A cryptocurrency can only be spent once and it can only have one owner at a time. If a cryptocurrency is claimed by two individuals at one time, then the ledger technology will process at most one ownership. This reduces the chances of double spending of a cryptocurrency to almost zero.

Characteristics of cryptocurrency: decentralized, immutable, portable, trustless, generally volatile, not yet a legal tender in many jurisdictions.

Characteristics of money: legal tender, durability, portability, divisibility, uniformity, limited supply, has intrinsic value and acceptability.

Cryptocurrencies are based on decentralized systems and typically are not issued or monitored by anybody. The ledger technology officially known as blockchain is self-sustaining. Blockchain is a decentralized technology spread across many computers that manages and records transactions. Blockchain has the ability to secure transaction records, control creation of new or additional coins and to verify transfer of coin membership. The fact that cryptocurrencies are decentralized, makes it hard for governments to regulate them.

Are cryptocurrencies popular? According to coinmarket.com there are at least 7121 cryptocurrencies with a market cap of $346,980,913,953 US dollars. All cryptocurrencies combined though account for less than 0.7% of world money. The use of cryptocurrencies is rising rapidly due to its perceived huge returns, but some argue that cryptocurrency is just a bubble.

The most popular altcoins as at September 2020 include Bitcoin (BTC), Ethereum (ETH), Tether, XRP, Bitcoin Cash (BCH), Polkadot (DOT), Binance Coin (BNB), Litecoin (LTC), Cardano (ADA), EOS, USD Coin (USDC), TRON (TRX), NEO, MONERO (XMR), Tezos (XTZ), Stellar (XML), NEM, DASH, Ethereum Classic (ETC), ZCash (ZEC), Dogecoin (DOGE) and Siacoin (SC).

Cryptocurrencies can be grouped into two subsets; namely Bitcoin and altcoins. Bitcoin (BTC) is often regarded as the first ever decentralized cryptocurrency and the most popular. As at 1217 h EAT on 21st September 2020, Bitcoin had an estimated dominance of 58.0% and market cap of $201,529,561,979 US dollars (www.coinmarket.com).

Altcoins, on the other hand represent all other cryptocurrencies apart from Bitcoin. Altcoins are alternatives to Bitcoin. Ideally, these are crypto coins which were launched after tremendous success of Bitcoin as a peer to peer digital currency. With the massive development of altcoins, distinct categories have evolved. Some of the main types of altcoins include mining-based cryptocurrencies, stable-coins, security tokens, and utility tokens.

Mining-based cryptocurrencies have the capability of generating new coins in a process popularly known as 'mining'. Mining involves solving challenging problems to unlock blocks and in the process a reward in form of cryptocurrency is given to the miners. Apart from Bitcoin, the other topmost mining-based altcoins as of September

2020 include Ethereum, Bitcoin Cash, Litecoin, Bitcoin SV, Cardano, Monero, Dash, Ethereum Classic, Zcash, DigiByte and Doge.

What is a crypto token? A crypto token is a special kind of cryptocurrency on the blockchain that represent a particular digital asset or utility. These altcoins are linked to a business, and they often launch in an initial coin offering (ICO). If a crypto token resembles traditional stocks and occasionally pay out some kind of dividend; then it is referred to as a security token. On the other hand, if crypto token provides a claim on services, and sometimes it is sold as part of the ICO; then it is a utility token. Stablecoins seek to stabilize the cryptocurrency market by reducing volatility of the crypto market. The value of these coins is usually tied to existing currencies or precious asset. The best example is Tether which is tied to the price of the USD.

The topmost crypto tokens in terms of market cap include Tether, ChainLink, Crypto.com Chain, UNUS SED LEO, yearn.finance, AAVE (EthLend), Maker, USD Coin, Theta Token, OmiseGO, Insight Chain, Basic Attention Token, Hedge Trade, Huobi Toekn, Ox, Loopring, TrueUSD, Paxos Standard Token, Flexacoin, Kyber Network, Auger, HUSD, Republic Protocol, Enjin Coin, OKB, Elrond, Quant, CyberVein, Ocean Protocol, KuCoin Shares, Golem, Status Network Token, Decentraland, Dai, iExec RLC, IOStoken, Crpto.com, Fantom, BitTorrent and Holo.

CHAPTER TWO

HISTORY OF CRYPTOCURRENCIES

Cryptocurrencies have a very rich history that dates back to early 1980s. It is paramount to point out that the growth of cryptocurrency heavily depends on the development and advancement of computer technology. Although Bitcoin is universally accepted as the first ever decentralized peer-to-peer cryptocurrency, but other cryptocurrency footprints existed before. This chapter has divided the history of cryptocurrency into five periods: before bitcoin (1980-2000), emergence of bitcoin (2001-2010), emergence of altcoins (2011-2015), tremendous rise in the price of bitcoin and altcoins (2016-2018), and the new crypto era (2019-present).

2.1 Before Bitcoin (1980-2000)

In 1983, David Chaum, an American Crystallographer conceived an anonymous cryptographic electronic money called ecash. In 1995, ecash was implemented through Digicash by Chaum himself. Digicash was used as a form of cryptographic electronic payment. This allowed the digital currency to be anonymous and untraceable. In 1998, Wei Dai published a description of "b-money", an anonymous, distributed electronic cash system. Shortly thereafter, Nick Szabo created "bit gold". Hal Finney later created a currency system based on reusable proof of work.

2.2 Emergence of Bitcoin (2001-2010)

Bitcoin is widely regarded as the first modern cryptocurrency – the first publicly used means of exchange to combine decentralized control, user anonymity, record-keeping via a blockchain, and built-in scarcity. It was first outlined in a 2008 white paper published by Satoshi Nakamoto, a pseudonymous bitcoin developer. In early 2009, Nakamoto released Bitcoin to the public, and a group of enthusiastic supporters began exchanging and mining the currency. Bitcoin used SHA-256, a cryptographic hash function, as its proof-of-work scheme.

Between January 2009 and March 2010, Bitcoin cost basically nothing. In March 2010, the price rose to 0.003 US dollars. In July 2010, its price sky-rocketed by 900% to trade between 0.008-0.08 US dollars.

Satoshi Nakamoto is a pseudonymous bitcoin developer.

In March 2010, first cryptocurrency exchange named bitcoinmarket.com (now defunct) appeared live to the public. In July the same year, Mt. Gox was launched as well. In 2 May 2010, the first recorded purchase of goods was made with Bitcoin when Laszlo Hanyecz bought two pizzas for 10,000 BTC (currently valued at over $115 M USD). Imagine buying two pizzas at $115 M USD!

2.3 Emergence of Altcoins (2011-2015)

Between February 2011 and April 2011, the price of one Bitcoin reached parity with 1 US dollar. In April 2013, the price rose to 266 US dollars. In November 2013, the price surpassed 1000 US dollars.

In April 2011, Namecoin was created as an attempt at forming a decentralized DNS, which would make internet censorship very difficult. Soon after, in October 2011, Litecoin was released. It was the first successful cryptocurrency to use scrypt as its hash function instead of SHA-256. Another notable cryptocurrency, Peercoin was the first to use a proof-of-work/proof-of-stake hybrid. IOTA was the first cryptocurrency not based on a blockchain, and instead uses the Tangle.

In June 2011, Mt.Gox got hacked for the first time and 2,000 BTC valued at $30,000 USD at that time was stolen. In 2013 Mt.Gox became the largest cryptocurrency exchange, at its peak handling 70% of all Bitcoin transactions. In February 2014, Mt.Gox again was hacked and lost 850,000 BTC valued at $ 460 M USD at that time.

In late 2012, WordPress became the first major merchant to accept payment in Bitcoin. Others, including Newegg.com, Expedia, and Microsoft, followed. According to Crypto ATM Radar, there are over 7000 bitcoin ATMs worldwide with USA having the majority. Merchants now view the world's most popular cryptocurrency as a legitimate payment method.

In 2012, a crypto asset known as Ripple (XRP), now ranked position 4 on Coinmarket, was released. Ripple was created for real-time gross settlement, currency exchange and remittance. It is built upon a distributed open source protocol. It supports tokens representing fiat currency, cryptocurrency, commodities or other units of value. In 2013, banks started having interest in using Ripple system in their payment systems.

In February 2014, MT. Gox, the world's largest cryptocurrency exchange at that time, declared bankruptcy. The company stated that it had lost nearly $473 million of their customer's bitcoins due to theft. The collapse of MT. Gox and other factors led to a big fall in the price of bitcoin to about $200 in March 2015.

In February 2014, MT. Gox, declared bankruptcy.

On 30th July 2015, The Ethereum network, currently the number 2 crypto asset in terms of market capitalization, was launched. It was developed by Ethereum Foundation but its original authors were Vitalik Buterin and Gavin Wood. Ethereum brought smart contracts to the cryptocurrency world.

Still in 2015, a crypto asset known as Augur held the first ICO. Auger used the smart contract of Ethereum and thus joined a group of other crypto assets based on Ethereum smart contract. These coins were named ERC-20. More and more ERC-20 tokens have been created. By October 2019, there were over 200 000 ERC-20 tokens with a market capitalization. Currently, other smart contract protocols besides ERC-20 have been developed. These protocols include ERC-223, ERC-721, ERC-827 and ERC-884.

In 2015, Ethereum was launched and its smart contracts followed.

2.4 Tremendous Rise in the Price of Bitcoin and Altcoins (2016-2018)

2017 was surely the year that saw not just Bitcoin but also other coins to skyrocket. On 17th December 2017, Bitcoin cost 19, 783.06 US dollars. On 21st September 2020, one Bitcoin was trading at about 10,896.13 US dollars.

In 2017, Binance, which is currently among the largest cryptocurrency exchange was launched. Binance coin was also launched the same year in June.

2.5 The new Crypto era (2019-Present)

The year 2019 has witnessed many cryptocurrency attacks targeting mainly cryptocurrency exchanges. These hack attacks have led to huge losses in the cryptocurrency sector. The hackers are advancing their attacks day by day and they don't seem to stop any time soon.

This period has witnessed significant development in the cryptocurrency sector. The best example is issuance of banking license to Kraken, a cryptocurrency based in the USA in September 2020. The implication is that Kraken can now conduct itself as a bank in the USA. Another development worth mentioning is the planned release of Libra coin backed by FaceBook, a giant social media company.

Kraken was awarded a banking license in September 2020.

CHAPTER THREE

ANALYSIS OF CRYPTOCURRENCIES

This chapter provides a deeper understanding of top 20 cryptocurrencies as at September 2020 based on their market cap. Data used in this analysis was based on www.coinmarket.com on 21st September 2020. All costs are quoted in US dollars.

Table 3.1: Analysis of Bitcoin and Ethereum

Rank	1	2
Name	Bitcoin	Ethereum
Symbol	BTC	ETH
ROI	7,728.38%	> 9000%
Market Cap	201,529,561,979	41,481,591,470
Current Price	10,896.13	368.11
All Time Low	65.53 (Jul 05, 2013)	0.420897 (Oct 21, 2015)
All Time High	20,089.00 (Dec 17, 2017)	1,432.88 (Jan 13, 2018)
Mineable	Yes	Yes

Table 3.2: Analysis of Tether and XRP

Rank	3	4
Name	Tether	XRP
Sticker	USDT	XRP
ROI	0.11%	3,931.57%
Market Cap	15,198,063,978	10,978,389,734
Current Price	1.00	0.243735
All Time Low	0.0 (Sep 18, 2019)	0.002802 (Jul 07, 2014)
All Time High	1.21 (May 27, 2017	3.84 (Jan 04, 2018)
Mineable	No	No

Table 3.3: Analysis of Bitcoin Cash and Polkadot

Rank	5	6
Name	Bitcoin Cash	Polkadot
Sticker	BCH	DOT
ROI	-61.36%	47.96%
Market Cap	4,163,222,400	3,758,112,180
Current Price	224.75	4.41
All Time Low	75.03 (Dec 15, 2018)	2.69 (Aug 20, 2020)
All Time High	4,355.62 (Dec 20, 2017	6.84 (Sep 01, 2020
Mineable	Yes	No

Table 3.4: Analysis of Binance Coin and Chainlink

Rank	7	8
Name	Binance Coin	ChainLink
Sticker	BNB	LINK
ROI	> 9000%	5,525.24%
Market Cap	3,676,280,755	3,290,132,808
Current Price	25.46	9.40
All Time Low	0.096109 (Aug 01, 2017)	0.126297 (Sep 23, 2017)
All Time High	39.57 (Jun 22, 2019	19.85 (Aug 16, 2020)
Mineable	No	No

Table 3.5: Analysis of Crypto.com Coin and Litecoin

Rank	9	10
Name	Crypto.com Coin	Litecoin
Sticker	CRO	LTC

ROI	678.99%	911.49%
Market Cap	3,202,636,109	3,072,906,925
Current Price	0.158942	46.91
All Time Low	0.011487 (Dec 17, 2018)	1.11 (Jan 14, 2015)
All Time High	0.201749 (Aug 21, 2020)	375.29 (Dec 19, 2017)
Mineable	No	Yes

Table 3.6: Analysis of Bitcoin SV and Cardano

Rank	11	12
Name	Bitcoin SV	Cardano
Sticker	BSV	ADA
ROI	65.11%	268.52%
Market Cap	2,820,198,043	2,661,077,740
Current Price	152.27	0.085531
All Time Low	36.87 (Nov 23, 2018)	0.017354 USD (Oct 01, 2017)
All Time High	441.20 (Jan 14, 2020)	1.33 USD (Jan 04, 2018)
Mineable	Yes	Yes

Table 3.7: Analysis of EOS and USD Coin

Rank	13	14
Name	EOS	USD Coin
Sticker	EOS	USDC
ROI	146.40%	-0.33%
Market Cap	2,491,837,032	2,321,649,726
Current Price	2.66	1.00
All Time Low	0.480196 (Oct 23, 2017)	0.929222 (Mar 13, 2020)
All Time High	22.89 (Apr 29, 2018)	1.11 (Oct 15, 2018)

Mineable	No	No

Table 3.8: Analysis of TRON and Monero

Rank	15	16
Name	TRON	Monero
Sticker	TRX	XMR
ROI	1,122.29%	3,413.98%
Market Cap	1,918,854,511	1,641,276,007
Current Price	0.026777	92.71
All Time Low	0.001091 (Sep 15, 2017)	0.212967 (Jan 14, 2015)
All Time High	0.300363 (Jan 05, 2018)	495.84 (Jan 07, 2018)
Mineable	No	Yes

Table 3.9: Analysis of NEO and Tezos

Rank	17	18
Name	NEO	Tezos
Sticker	NEO	XTZ
ROI	> 9000%	312.23%
Market Cap	1,619,935,567	1,612,144,394
Current Price	22.97	2.17
All Time Low	0.072287 (Oct 21, 2016)	0.314631 (Dec 07, 2018)
All Time High	196.85 (Jan 15, 2018)	4.48 (Aug 13, 2020)
Mineable	No	No

CHAPTER FOUR

BLOCKCHAIN

Blockchain is no doubt one of the most outstanding inventions in modern human civilization. To begin with, think of common scenarios in our daily lives. An online store code-name 'XYZ' sells more than 200 different types of items. The shop has been in operation for about 5 years. Is there a way all transactions in this shop can be recorded seamlessly and without human interference? Is there a way anybody anywhere can access all transactions including the exact date and time? Is there a way for anybody anywhere to monitor the flow of stock, income and expenditure? Well, perhaps blockchain is the answer to these questions.

Simplistically, blockchain is a computer ledger containing a record of online transactions. It can also be defined as a decentralized, distributed ledger. The word 'Block' means digital information while 'Chain' means public database; therefore, blockchain is a technology that records immutable timestamped digital transactions that can be accessed by anybody or anyone anywhere.

> Blockchain is a computer ledger containing a record of online transactions.

Blocks on the blockchain store information about who is participating in the transaction (using unique digital signature), date, time, amount and 'hash' of the block. A 'hash' is a unique code that distinguishes one block from another. The size of a block depends on the number of transactions; one block alone can hold thousands of transactions.

Blockchain contains very many blocks and these blocks can be accessed by anyone for free. Each block contains transactions or digital information. How does blockchain work? How is a block added to blockchain? These and many other questions are always asked by blockchain newbies. Blockchain exists because there is a computer technology framework and transactions keep it going. For a block to be added to blockchain, transactions must be initiated and verified. People initiate transactions but verification is done by computer networks; perhaps a thousand or millions of computer networks. Once a transaction is verified, it is added to an available block at that particular time to join a list of other transactions. The block is assigned a unique code called hash and then added to end of the blockchain. Information on the block can now be accessed by anybody anywhere for free.

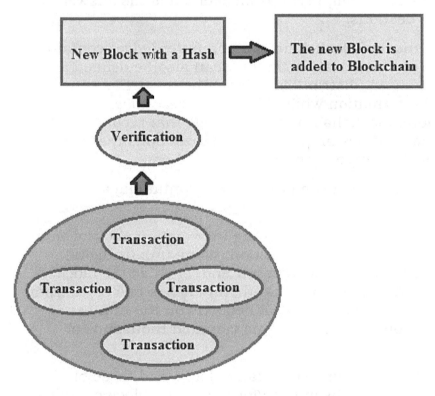

Figure 4.1: Validation of transactions in blockchain

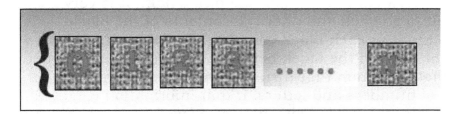

Figure 4.2: How new blocks are added to the blockchain

Blockchain is a public ledger therefore anyone can view its contents. However, computer users can also opt to connect their computers to the blockchain network as nodes. In doing so, their computers receive a copy of the blockchain that is updated automatically whenever a new block is added. Remember, a new block (N) is normally added at the end of the block. The blockchain does not close and keeps block after block.

Computers that want to join and add blocks to the chain must "prove" themselves before they can participate in a blockchain network. One of the most common examples employed by Bitcoin is called "proof of work." In the proof of work system, computers must "prove" that they have done "work" by solving a complex computational math problem. If a computer solves one of these problems, they become eligible to add a block to the blockchain. This process of adding blocks to blockchain networks by solving complex mathematical problems is referred to as mining in the cryptocurrency world.

Blockchain is regarded as very secure since it is almost impossible to alter a record on its network. By design, blockchains are inherently resistant to modification of the data. New blocks are always added at the 'end' of blockchain; that is, linearly and chronologically. Each block typically contains a hash pointer as a link to a previous block, a timestamp and transaction data.

Each block has a position called a 'height' and after a block has been added to the end of the blockchain, it is very difficult to go back and alter the contents of the block. That's because each block contains its own hash, along with the hash of the block before it. Hash codes are created by a math function that turns digital information into a string of numbers and letters. If that information is edited in any way, the hash code changes as well. Once recorded, the data in any given block cannot be altered retroactively without the alteration of all subsequent blocks, which requires collusion of the network majority.

Table 4.1 Recent Blocks (live.blockcypher.com) as at 12:50 pm EAT on 30th September 2020

Height	Age	Transactions	Block Size (in bytes)
650633	2020-09-30T09:40:51.923Z	2,729	909,800
650632	2020-09-30T09:06:31.503Z	2,252	911,050
650631	2020-09-30T09:04:09.523Z	2,200	923,358
650630	2020-09-30T08:55:51.339Z	2,526	877,507
650629	2020-09-30T08:54:27.673Z	2,990	893,388

Cryptocurrencies use various timestamping schemes to "prove" the validity of transactions added to the blockchain ledger without the need for a trusted third party. The first timestamping scheme invented was the proof-of-work scheme. The most widely used proof-of-work schemes are based on SHA-256 and scrypt. Some other hashing algorithms that are used for proof-of-work include SHA-3, and X11.

The proof-of-stake is a method of securing a cryptocurrency network and achieving distributed consensus through requesting users to show ownership of a certain amount of currency. It is different from proof-of-work systems that run difficult hashing algorithms to validate electronic transactions. The scheme is largely dependent on the coin, and there is currently no standard form of it. Some cryptocurrencies use a combined proof-of-work and proof-of-stake scheme.

The Bitcoin protocol is built on the blockchain. All transactions involving transfer of bitcoins from one person or entity to another are recorded in bitcoin blockchain. In order to conduct transactions on the Bitcoin network, participants must run a program called a "wallet." Each wallet consists of two unique and distinct cryptographic keys: a public key and a private key. The public key is the location or address where bitcoins are deposited to and withdrawn from. This is also the key that appears on the blockchain ledger as the user's digital signature. When person A sends bitcoins to person B, computer network will verify the transaction and then the transaction is added to a block. The block is assigned a unique code called hash; once successful, the block is added to blockchain. The recipient normally receives bitcoins in their digital wallets after a few verifications.

A private key is 'private' and therefore the only person who should know it is the respective owner. You need private key to withdraw coins from your public key. If your private keys end up in wrong hands, then you might lose your coins. Do not share your private key- that is your most guarded secret.

Do not share your wallet private key with anyone.

CHAPTER FIVE

MINING

In cryptocurrency networks, mining is a validation or verification of transactions. It involves adding new data blocks to blockchain by solving complex mathematical problems. Computer users otherwise called miners connect their computers to blockchain of mineable cryptocurrencies and assist in validating transactions. Successful miners are rewarded cryptocurrencies for their work.

In cryptocurrency networks, mining is a validation or verification of transactions.

The reward decreases transaction fees by creating a complementary incentive to contribute to the processing power of the network. The rewards paid to miners increase the supply of the cryptocurrency. The verification algorithm requires a lot of processing power, this translates to huge electricity consumption. The mining machines also generate a lot of heat and hence need constant cooling to keep the process running smoothly. The miners also have to factor in the costs associated with expensive equipment necessary to stand a chance of solving a hash problem.

The rate of generating hashes, which validates blockchain transaction, has been increased by the use of specialized machines such as ASICs running complex hashing algorithms like SHA-256 and Scrypt. With more people entering the world of cryptocurrency, generating hashes for this validation has become far more complex over the years, with miners having to invest huge sums of money on multiple high-performance ASICs. Thus, the value of the currency obtained for finding a hash often does not justify the amount of money spent on setting up the machines, the cooling facilities to overcome the heat they produce, and the electricity required to run them. Cryptocurrency mining has thus become a costly undertaking.

Some miners pool resources, sharing their processing power over a network to split the reward equally, according to the amount of work they contributed to the probability of finding a block. An award commensurate to the miner's work is awarded to members of the mining pool who present a valid pow.

> By 27th September 2020, the network difficulty was 19.315 trillion times!

Mining cryptocurrency is no longer a lucrative business because of high costs associated with it. But most importantly, mining difficulty has increased sharply and the chances (or odds) of getting a mining reward is extremely low. In fact, as at 27th September 2020, the network difficulty was 19.315 trillion times! (www.blockchain.com).

Mining of cryptocurrency has also been infiltrated by mining scams such as bitconnect and quartercore.co (both defunct). Others are bitcoindoubler.club and cryptomia247. There are over a million bitcoin scams waiting for gullible 'investors' to pounce on. These mining frauds trick their gullible targets into buying into their non-existent mining plans only to run away with their hard-earned cash. These fake cloud mining companies also known as bitcoin hyips, usually lure their 'preys' with unimaginable profits such as doubling bitcoins within 24 hours, 2% profit per day, lifetime mining contracts, fake ICOs, among other fake niceties. Beware! 99.99% of bitcoin mining is fraud. There is nothing like legit bitcoin hyips-all these are absolute scams and will run away with your money before you realize it.

> Beware of fake bitcoin mining scams.

CHAPTER SIX

CRYPTOCURRENCY EXCHANGES

Cryptocurrency exchanges are simply 'markets' where cryptocurrencies are traded. They operate just like a typical market where buyers and sellers meet to transact their business. Binance, Coinbase Pro, Kraken, Bittrex and Bitstamp are among the most popular cryptocurrency exchanges. Besides buying and selling cryptocurrencies, some exchanges also offer trading futures and loans.

To transact a trade on any exchange, a customer is required to register and verify their identity. Some exchanges allow trading without verification but most centralized exchanges such as Kraken, Binance, Bittrex and Coinbase run rigorous KYC (Know Your Client) procedures; requiring customers to provide their identity card issued by their respective jurisdictions.

Customers are normally charged transaction fees for transacting on the exchange. Some exchanges charge very low fees, others charge high fees; although, a few do not charge any transaction fees. Binance currently is the most popular cryptocurrency in the world while Coinbase is a well-established and regulated exchanged in the United States of America.

6.1 Binance

The Binance is a cryptocurrency exchange established in 2017 with a strong focus on altcoin trading. Currently, it is the most popular cryptocurrency exchange in the world with a web traffic factor of 1000. Binance offers about 600 different trading pairs between different cryptocurrencies. It also offers some fiat/crypto pairs, but most of its pairs are between cryptocurrencies. It offers a large variety of cryptocurrencies and trading pairs. Above all, it has a more advanced trading chart.

Bitcoin has lower trading fees than other commonly used exchanges. Current fees stand at 0.1% for the taker and 0.1% for the maker. Using Binance's native cryptocurrency, BNB, lowers fees by 50%. It is free to deposit any cryptocurrency on its platform but charges 0.0005 BTC for BTC withdrawal and 0.01 ETH for ETH withdrawal.

Binance also offers over 20 fiat currencies for deposits, excluding USD. A customer can also purchase cryptocurrencies with a credit or debit card.

6.2 Coinbase

Coinbase is the most widely known and used cryptocurrency exchange in the United States. It was founded in 2012 and is fully regulated and licensed to operate in the USA. Currently it is licensed to operate in over 40 USA states and territories. Coinbase is very secure and has a simple interface. Its main cons include higher fees, fewer coins and geographical limitation.

6.3 Coinbase Pro

Coinbase Pro (formerly GDAX) is among the most popular cryptocurrency exchanges with a web traffic factor of 959 and average liquidity of 388. It has a simple interface and supports at least 15 coins. The cons of Coinbase Pro include fewer altcoins and geographical limitation. Furthermore, the user does not control wallet keys.

6.4 Comparison of Some Popular Cryptocurrency Exchanges

Table 6.1: Binance, Huobi Global and Coinbase Pro

Rank	1	2	3
Name	Binance	Huobi Global	Coinbase Pro
Web Traffic Factor (out of 1000)	1000	780	959

Avg Liquidity	466	502	388
Coins Supported	150	184	At least 15
Countries Accepted	Global	Global	100+
Launched	July 2017	September 2013	May 2014
Registration	Yes	Yes	Yes
KYC	ID required	ID	ID required
User level	Intermediate	Intermediate	Basic
Fiat	Supported but not USD	Supported	Supported
Security of coins	Very secure	Secure	Very secure

Table 6.2: Kraken, Bithumb and Bitfnex

Rank	4	5	6
Name	Kraken	Bithumb	Bitfnex
Web Traffic Factor (out of 1000)	856	809	771
Avg Liquidity	390	184	421
Coins Supported	Many	Many	Many
Countries Accepted	Global	Global	Global
Launched	July 2011	January 2014	October 2012
Registration	Yes	Yes	Yes
KYC	Yes	Yes	Yes
Security of coins	Very secure	Secure	Secure

Table 6.3: ZB.COM, bitFlyer and Upbit

Rank	7	8	9
Name	ZB.COM	BitFlyer	Upbit
Web Traffic Factor (out of 1000)	1000	780	959
Avg Liquidity	466	502	388
Coins Supported	Many	Many	Many
Countries Accepted	Global	Global	Global
Launched	November 2017	January 2014	October 2017
Registration	Yes	Yes	Yes
KYC	Yes	Yes	Yes
Security of coins	Secure	Secure	Secure

Table 6.4: Bittrex, Bitstamp and Coinone

Rank	10	11	12
Name	Bittrex	Bitstamp	Coinone
Web Traffic Factor (out of 1000)	848	792	707
Avg Liquidity	205	225	193
Coins Supported	235	5	125
Countries Accepted	Global	Global	Global
Launched	February 2014	July 2011	June 2014
Registration	Yes	Yes	Yes

KYC	Yes	Yes	Yes
Security of coins	Secure	Secure	Secure

Table 6.5: Comparison of Coins, Markets and Trading Fees

No	Exchange	#Cryptos	#Markets	Maker Fee	Taker Fee
1	Binance	150	439	0.1%	0.1%
2	Huobi Global	184	412	0.2%	0.2%
3	Coinbase Pro	16	35	0.0%	0.3%
4	Kraken	20	73	0.16%	0.26%
5	Bittrex	235	328	0.25%	0.25%
6	Bithumb	78	78	0.15%	0.15%
7	Bitfnex	101	285	0.1%	0.1%
8	ZB.COM	64	122	0.2%	0.2%
9	Bitflyer	3	3	0.15%	0.15%
10	Bitstamp	5	14	0.25%	0.25%
11	Coinone	125	62	0.20%	0.20%

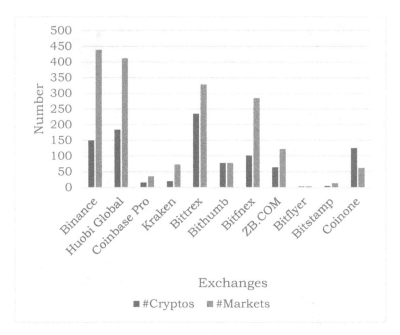

Graph 6.1: Comparison of number of coins and markets

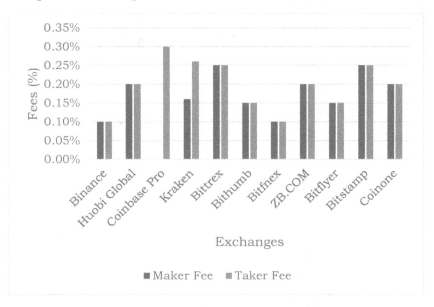

Graph 6.2: Comparison of trading fees

Table 6.5: Comparison of Deposit and Withdrawal Fees

No	Exchange	Deposit Fees		Withdrawal Fees	
		BTC	ETH	BTC	ETH
1	Binance	0.0	0.0	0.0005	0.01
2	Huobi Global	0.0	0.0	0.0005	0.005
3	Coinbase Pro	0.0	0.0	0.0	0.0
4	Kraken	0.0	0.0	0.0005	0.005
5	Bittrex	0.0	0.0	0.0005	0.006
6	Bithumb	0.0	0.0	0.001	0.01
7	Bitfnex	0.0004	0.00135	0.0004	0.00135
8	ZB.COM	0.0	0.0	0.001	0.01
9	Bitflyer	0.0	0.0	0.0004	0.005
10	Bitstamp	0.0	0.0	0.0	0.0
11	Coinone	0.0	0.0	0.0015	0.02

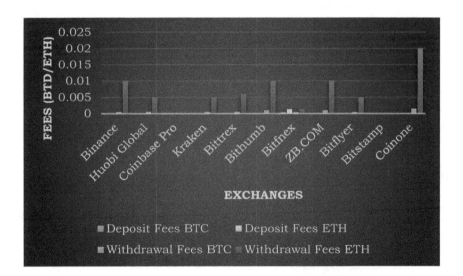

Graph 6.3: Comparison of Deposit and Withdrawal Fees

Table 6.6: Comparison of Hack Attacks in 2019

No	Exchange	#Attacks	Date	Amount (USD)
1	Binance	1	7 May 2019	40 M
2	Huobi Global	0	None	-
3	Coinbase Pro	0	None	-
4	Kraken	0	None	-
5	Bittrex	0	None	-
6	Bithumb	1	30 March 2019	18.7 M
7	Bitfnex	0	None	-
8	ZB.COM	0	None	-
9	Bitflyer	0	None	-
10	Bitstamp	0	None	-
11	Coinone	0	None	-

CHAPTER SEVEN

ADVANTAGES OF CRYPTOCURRENCY

7.1 Privacy of Transactions

Cryptocurrencies hold the promise of making it easier to transfer funds directly between two parties, without the need for a trusted third party like a bank or credit card company. These transfers are instead secured by the use of public keys and private keys and different forms of incentive systems, like pow or pos.

7.2 Strong Security

Cryptocurrency transactions are immutable meaning they cannot be reversed once authorized. Furthermore, the strong encryption techniques employed throughout blockchain and cryptocurrency transaction processes are a safeguard against fraud and account attack.

7.3 No Middlemen

Cryptocurrency transactions are peer-to-peer hence cuts out middlemen and other complications hence reducing transaction fees and time of transaction.

7.4 Low Transaction Fees

Cryptocurrency transactions are peer-to-peer, meaning middlemen and third-parties are cut out completely. There is nothing like negotiation fees. As a result, transaction fees tend to be lower and cannot be inflated.

7.5 Access to Loans

Digital assets can be used as collateral to access credit while maintaining your cryptocurrency portfolio. Already there are cryptocurrency platforms and exchanges such as Bankera offering loans to their customers with cryptocurrencies as collateral.

7.6 Enhanced International Trade

International trade is obviously hindered by funds transfer. The existing mainstream funds transfer systems are very expensive, complicated and time consuming. But using peer-to-peer blockchain technology, international trade can be enhanced to unimaginable levels. There will be no application of exchange rates, double processing fees and other levies.

7.7 Savings/ investment scheme

Cryptocurrencies can be bought and held as savings or investment. Even mainstream financial institutions cannot be entirely trusted with your funds, so investing in cryptocurrency, though a gamble but can give you huge profits in the long run.

CHAPTER EIGHT

DISADVANTAGES OF CRYPTOCURRENCY

8.1 Cyber Crimes and Terrorism

As the popularity of cryptocurrencies soars due to increased demand, so are the concerns that cryptocurrencies may become tools for anonymous web criminals and terrorism.

8.2 Tax Evasion and Money Laundering

Cryptocurrency networks display a marked lack of regulation that attracts many users who seek decentralized exchange and use of currency; however, the very same lack of regulations has been criticized as potentially enabling criminals who seek to engage in money laundering and tax evasion.

8.3 Fake ICOs

The cryptocurrencies have opened floodgates of scrupulous funds sourcing popularly known as ICOs (Initial Coin Offering). An ICO is used by startups to bypass rigorous and regulated capital-raising processes required by venture capitalists or banks. Some of these ICOs end up us scams leading to loss of funds by their contributors and backers.

8.4 Legality

The legal status of cryptocurrencies varies from country to country and is still undefined or changing in many of them. While some countries have given a green light to use and trade with bitcoin, others have banned or restricted it.

8.5 Evasion of Economic Sanctions

Cryptocurrencies are a potential tool to evade economic sanctions. A country can still benefit financially from its allies even with international economic sanctions.

8.6 Theft

Cryptocurrencies are prone to loss, theft, and fraud. In February 2014 the world's largest bitcoin exchange, Mt. Gox, declared bankruptcy. On 21 November 2017, the Tether cryptocurrency announced they were hacked, losing $31 million in USDT from their primary wallet. In June 2018, Korean exchange Coinrail was hacked, losing US$37 million worth of altcoin. On 9 July 2018 the exchange Bancor lost $23.5 million in cryptocurrency to hackers.

8.7 Volatility

Since market prices for cryptocurrencies are based on supply and demand, the rate at which a cryptocurrency can be exchanged for another currency can fluctuate widely, since the design of many cryptocurrencies ensures a high degree of scarcity. Bitcoin has experienced some rapid surges and collapses in value, climbing as high as $19,000 per Bitcoin in Dec. of 2017 before dropping to around $7,000 in the subsequent months. Some economists consider cryptocurrencies as a short-lived fad or speculative bubble that burst any time.

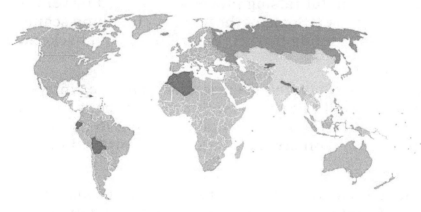

Figure

Figure 8.1: Worldmap showing legality status (www.wikipedia.com)

Green		Permissive (legal to use bitcoin)
Red		Hostile (full or partial restriction)
Yellow		Contentious (some legal restrictions on usage of bitcoin)
Pink		Contentious (interpretation of old laws, but bitcoin is not prohibited directly).
Grey		No data

CHAPTER NINE

MAJOR CRYPTOCURRENCY ATTACKS

The success of cryptocurrencies is obviously derailed by constant hacks and scams across the crypto world leading to huge losses. www.thebalance.com identified five common bitcoin scams that people should be wary of. These scams are; i. Fake bitcoin exchanges, ii. Ponzi schemes or pyramid schemes, iii. Fake Cryptocurrencies, iv. Old school scams and v. Malware. Some of the worst cryptocurrency attacks are described below;

9.1 Coincheck: $534 Million

In January 2018, the Japanese exchange Coincheck lost 523 million NEM coins valued at about $534 million in a hack attack.

9.2 MT.Gox $450 million

From 2013 until 2014, MT.GOX managed over 70% of all Bitcoin transactions in the world. In February 2014, Mt. Gox suspended the transactions, closed the site and declared itself bankrupt after losing over 744,408 Bitcoins valued at about $450 million to hackers.

9.3 BitGrail: $195 Million

In February 2018, Italian exchange BitGrail claimed it had lost $195 million in the token Nano.

9.4 NiceHash: $64 Million

Slovenian-based Bitcoin mining marketplace, NiceHash, launched in 2014, lost approximately 4,700 Bitcoins worth about $64 million in a hack.

9.5 Zaif: $60.0 Million

In 2018, Korean Zaif Exchange lost $60 million through a hot wallet attack. Bitcoin, Bitcoin Cash, and MonaCoin were stolen through this attack.

9.6 Coinrail: $37.2 Million

Coinrail, a South Korean lost $37.2 million of digital assets in a 2018 attack by hackers.

9.7 Bithumb: $31.5 Million

In 2018, Bithumb, a Korean exchange, suffered a $31.5 million theft.

9.8 Bitpoint: $27.9 Million

In July, cryptocurrency exchange Bitpoint revealed loss of $27.9 million through a hack attack.

9.9 Bittrex: $18 Million

Bittrex, a USA cryptocurrency exchange and one of the largest in the world, suffered a series of hacking attacks that led to the loss of over $18 million in funds. Biticoin Gold Coin (now dropped from Bittrex exchange) was the culprit for the attacks.

9.10 Cryptsy: $9.5 Million

In early 2016, Cryptsy exchange suffered an attack in which 13.00 BTC and 300,000 LTC were stolen, for a total value of $9.5 million. The attack occurred through the insertion of a Trojan malware within the code that allowed the cyber-criminal to reach sensitive information and transfer cryptocurrencies.

CHAPTER TEN

THE FUTURE OF CRYPTOCURRENCY

10.0 Introduction

Bitcoins and other altcoins still face a herculean task of circumventing their way to full adoption. First, there is an issue of legality of Bitcoins. Many local governments have put tight restrictions on Cryptocurrencies while others have banned them completely.

Bitcoin's main benefits of decentralization and transaction anonymity have also made it a favored currency for a host of illegal activities including money laundering, drug peddling, smuggling and weapons procurement

The process of validating blocks in blockchain technology popularly known as mining, consumes a lot of electricity and also require constant cooling. Cryptocurrency mining has been found to be a significant environmental pollutant. Mining has also become difficult and now a lot of money is used to invest in very expensive mining equipment.

Constant hacking attacks targeted at cryptocurrency exchanges have led to huge losses to the exchanges and their clients. Protection of cryptocurrency in hot wallets, cold wallets and cryptocurrency exchanges is an irreducible minimum for people's trust in cryptocurrencies.

Most cryptocurrencies, of course with the exception of stable-coins are very volatile and can lead to huge losses within minutes. To understand the gravity of volatile nature of cryptocurrencies, take a scenario of an 'investor' who buys 10 bitcoins at $12000 USD per bitcoin; which amounts to $120000 USD. Suppose the price of one bitcoin drops to $8000 USD overnight, then that person's portfolio will drop to $80000 USD; this translates to a loss of $40000 USD.

The future of cryptocurrency depends heavily on overcoming these challenges. Of course, legalization of cryptocurrencies in many territories will most likely push cryptocurrencies to another level. Based on the history of cryptocurrency and prevailing conditions, the following are possible scenarios or speculations about cryptocurrency.

10.1 Legalization in many territories

Legality of cryptocurrencies is perhaps the major challenge cryptocurrencies are facing. However, if stakeholders, experts and backers of cryptocurrencies can convince local authorities on the operation-ability, security and benefits of cryptocurrencies, then more and more territories could consider legalizing cryptocurrencies.

10.2 Integration in the banking sector

A cryptocurrency that aspires to become part of the mainstream financial system may have to satisfy widely divergent criteria. It would need to be mathematically complex to avoid fraud and hacker attacks but easy for consumers to understand. It needs to be decentralized but with adequate consumer safeguards and protection. It would also need to preserve user anonymity without providing a leeway for money laundering, tax evasion, terrorism, drug dealing, smuggling and other antisocial activities.

With increased adoption of cryptocurrencies coupled by legalization in some nations, cryptocurrencies are slowly creeping into the banking sector. In September 2020, Kraken, a huge cryptocurrency platform based in the USA was awarded a special purpose depository institution (SPDI) charter by the state of Wyoming; making it one of the banks in the USA. Kraken will have to abide by the Wyoming law which requires it to maintain 100% reserves of its deposits of fiat currency at all times. Kraken plans to be a global bank in future.

10.3 Listing on Stock Exchanges

There is the possibility that cryptocurrencies will be floated on mainstream major stock markets such as Nasdaq, this would further add credibility to blockchain and its uses as an alternative to conventional currencies.

10.4 Bitcoin ATMs and Merchant Shops

Jordan Kelley, founder of Robocoin, launched the first bitcoin ATM in the United States on February 20, 2014. Many bitcoin ATMs have been installed so far with majority based in the USA. According to www.coinatmradar.com , by September 2020, there were 10398 Crypto ATMs in 71 countries around the world. With this trend, the number of crypto ATMs worldwide is set to surge immensely.

While the number of merchants who accept cryptocurrencies has steadily increased, still there is much to be done to increase acceptability of bitcoins and altcoins globally. For cryptocurrencies to become more widely used, they have to first gain widespread acceptance among consumers. However, their relative complexity compared to conventional currencies will likely deter most people, except for the technologically adept. But with modernization and technological advancement, transactions involving cryptocurrencies might become user friendly-meaning more people will be willing to adopt them.

10.5 Stablecoins

Stablecoins are cryptocurrencies designed to minimize the volatility of the price of the cryptocurrencies. A stablecoin can be pegged to a cryptocurrency, fiat money, or to exchange-traded commodities. Such coins are said to be backed while those pegged to an algorithm are referred to as seigniorage-style (not backed).

Cryptocurrency backed stablecoins are issued with cryptocurrencies as collateral on the blockchain, using smart contracts in a more decentralized fashion. The value of fiat-backed stablecoins is based on the value of the backing currency, which is held by a third-party regulated financial institution. Best examples include Tether which is backed by the $ USD and upcoming Libra coin backed by FaceBook. Commodity backed stablecoins are backed by the value of commodities such as precious metals (gold, silver etc.) and oil. These coins are less more likely to be inflated than all other stable coins. Since stable coins are not volatile on the market, their adoption and utilization in various sectors may be attractive.

10.6 Creation of Cryptocurrencies on major social media platforms

With FaceBook's crypto-asset named Libra in the pipeline; perhaps other major social media platforms may jump the bandwagon and start their own cryptocurrencies.

10.7 Surge in the number of crypto coins

Currently, there are over 7000 cryptocurrencies and more are being created. This trend may not stop soon.

10.8 Surge in the price of bitcoin and altcoins

Bitcoin's curve since its inception shows an upward trajectory. Even if there are drops here and there, sometimes huge, but generally the price shows an upward trend. It is predicted that the price of bitcoin will surge past $100000 USD mark in future. It sounds like a dream but it is possible. Remember at one time one bitcoin cost nothing but went on to rise up to $ 20000 USD in 2018. Given that many altcoins except stablecoin depend on the behavior of bitcoin, chances are that the price of those altcoins will also rise. However, a huge fall or even a complete wipe-out of cryptocurrencies cannot be overlooked.

10.9 Increased attacks and scams

As long as people with ill motives exist, attacks on cryptocurrency exchanges and cryptocurrency wallets will not end any time soon. In fact, it is predicted that attacks will increase with increased adoption of cryptocurrencies. To rebuff the attacks, which mostly lead to loss of funds, cryptocurrency exchanges will have to advance their security systems. Cryptocurrency holders should also be educated or sensitized on best practices when dealing with cryptocurrencies.

CHAPTER ELEVEN

HOW TO BUY AND SELL BITCOINS

Buying and selling bitcoins has never been easy to cryptocurrency newbies. This is a delicate part and any mistake will make you lose your funds. In this regard, this chapter gives a detailed guide on how to buy and sell bitcoins on selected cryptocurrency exchanges (Kraken & Localbitcoins). However, make sure you understand the legality of cryptocurrencies in your jurisdiction.

11.1 Localbitcoins

Banks in many jurisdictions do not allow their customers to transact bitcoins using their bank accounts. Some banks will unceremoniously lock your bank account once they discover that you received funds from a bitcoin source. This is where Localbitcoins comes in. Localbitcoins is a peer-to-peer cryptocurrency platform which allows its customers to buy and sell bitcoins using payment gateways available in each country.

One only needs to sign up on localbitcoins official website and can start buying and selling bitcoins. However, to increase your credibility, you need to verify your account with a Government issued ID in your jurisdiction.

To buy bitcoins, navigate to buy tab then enter your country and currency. Select your preferred method of payment and click search. A market showing potential sellers and their respective price per bitcoin will be displayed. A green dot implies the seller is online/ available and ready to trade. A yellow dot means the seller is not available. A grey dot means the customer is not selling; perhaps on vacation.

Click on the suitable seller (with a green dot), preferably one offering lower bitcoin price but be sure to check their percent rating first-anything less than 100% is questionable. Enter the number of bitcoins you wish to buy or better still, the amount of money you wish to spend and click buy. Ensure you read the customer's terms and conditions before you proceed with the transaction. Wait for the seller to send payment details in chat section; some sellers indicate payment details in their terms of trade. Once you receive payment details, go ahead and pay. You may copy-paste the payment message in the chat area as proof of payment. Wait for the seller to release bitcoins. Credible will release bitcoins almost immediately. Remember as soon as you initiate buy process, the sellers bitcoins equivalent to your funds are secured by escrow. The escrow protects you from being scammed. There you go! You now have your first bitcoin in your wallet. Go back and check your wallet, be sure to see some bitcoins in your wallet.

Selling bitcoins on localbitcoins is also as easy as buying. Click the sell bitcoins tab and select your country and currency. Look for buyers offering a higher price but ensure they are online and also have a credible record. Enter the number of bitcoins you wish to sell, enter your payment details and some comments (optional) and click send. At this stage, your bitcoins will be moved to escrow until you release to your buyer. Wait for the buyer to pay and then release bitcoins. If you have enabled a two-factor protection, then you will be required to enter an OTP (one-time passcode) generated by your authenticator (such as google authenticator) to complete the trade. Ensure you have received funds before you release escrow otherwise you may lose your bitcoins.

Besides in-country payment gateways, cross-border methods such as PayPal can also be used to transact on localbitcoins platform. Payment via PayPal is fast and easy, you only require an email to send or receive funds if you are already registered with PayPal. The cons of using PayPal on Localbitcoins include higher transaction fees and increased chances of being scammed. PayPal itself is very secure but using it on Localbitcoins platform might expose you to fraudsters.

As much as localbitcoins is a very popular peer-to-peer bitcoin platform, but its safety is not guaranteed. You can lose your money or bitcoins on localbitcoins to scammers. Only transact with verified clients with an unquestionable credibility rating (100%). Privacy of customers is not guaranteed since the mode of transactions is peer-to-peer. This exposes customers to cyber-attacks, bullying, scams and many other ills.

Before you start engaging in bitcoins business, define your purpose first. Do you want to be a day trader? Do you want to buy and hold? Do you want to buy and invest in mining? These are some of the investment questions you need to ask yourself. Day trading can be tricky to a newbie because you need on-hand skills and experience first. Otherwise you will end up with huge loses; perhaps you may lose everything. Learn bitcoin environment first before you become a day trader.

Buying and holding can be lucrative but needs a lot of patience- you may wait for a long time to realize a nice profit. Buying and holding has created bitcoin millionaires and billionaires but you have to be carefully when investing in this plan.

Bitcoin mining is no longer lucrative. If you decide to mine alone with your mining machines, you may never earn any bitcoin reward. Perhaps, you may join pool mining with your mining machines but still rewards are meagre considering the high-end equipment needed for mining, high cost of electricity and constant cooling of mining machines.

For those who cannot run their own mining machines, cloud mining is an alternative. Cloud mining is offered by mining companies who rent their mining machines to customers at a fee. The cloud companies have investment plans from which a customer selects and pays upfront. The plans can run for one year, 2 years or even lifetime. Your profits will be deposited into your account from time to time. You may withdraw your bitcoins to your wallet once a threshold amount (minimum withdrawable amount) is reached.

Most of cloud mining companies are however not credible. In fact, 99.99% of bitcoin cloud mining companies are absolute scams. You invest your money and they run away with it; leaving you bruised financially. A few like Genesis and Hashflare have stood the test of time and they are still offer mining plans, although not profitable at all.

11.2 Kraken

To transact on Kraken, you need to register and verify your account. Kraken has a variety of payment gateways which include international wire transfer, SEPA, bitcoin and other altcoins. You need to send funds into your account to buy bitcoins on Kraken. You may use international wire transfer, credit card or SEPA to deposit funds your fiat account and then use the funds to purchase bitcoins. If you do not want to use mainstream banking system to deposit money into fiat Kraken account, then purchase bitcoins on peer-to-peer platforms such as Localbitcoins and send to your Kraken account. You can also request a friend or a family to deposit bitcoins into your Kraken account and then pay them by cash. You need a bitcoin address (a unique code consisting of alphanumeric) to receive bitcoins. This code is not private and can be shared.

You can also sell your bitcoins and receive fiat into your Kraken account. Bitcoin allows you to leverage your trades up to 5×. For instance, you have $2000 USD worthy of bitcoins in your account then you can leverage your funds up to $10000 USD on the market. Once the trade is completed, Kraken recovers leverage funds and all fees.

Leveraging can be lucrative but at the same time highly risky. he funds in fiat can then be transferred to your bank using international bank wire and SEPA. You may also send your bitcoins into a peer-to-peer platform and sell there.

CHAPTER TWELVE

CONCLUSION

Invention of blockchain is perhaps one of the major breakthroughs of mankind. Bitcoin is built on the bedrock of blockchain. The emergence of Bitcoin undoubtedly has engineered a revolution in the financial sector. No one knows the future of bitcoins and other altcoins. The society is fast accepting cryptocurrencies even with the question of legality still lingering. Full adoption of cryptocurrencies is still in jeopardy since cryptocurrencies are much more complex than fiat currencies. The society should be made to understand how blockchain and cryptocurrencies work.

Generally, one can invest in cryptocurrency through trading, holding (HODL), mining and cloud mining. Trading involves buying and selling cryptocurrency regularly by taking advantage of constant swings in the value of cryptocurrencies. This is rather speculative and possibly dangerous. Holding looks like a better prospect to some investors-simply buy and hold (hodl) and sell when the price peaks or at their convenience.

If you are considering investing in cryptocurrencies in whichever way, think about it again. It looks lucrative but again it is a speculative venture and your investment might be wiped out in matter of hours or even minutes. Bitcoin is susceptible to huge price swings and if you cannot afford losing your hard-earned cash, then look for another investment. However, if you have to invest, then do not invest your life savings, fortune, school fees or funds belonging to another entity. Ensure you understand basics of cryptocurrencies and blockchain. If you buy coins for holding, then be advised to store them in a cold wallet and never share your private keys. Cryptocurrency exchanges are prone to attacks and your coins may not be safe idling there.

It is not all gloom with bitcoin and cryptocurrencies. There are very many success stories surrounding cryptocurrencies. Talk of someone who bought 1000 bitcoins for a paltry $3 USD in 2010 and now that value of one bitcoin is about $12000 USD, do the mathematics. His value in bitcoins would be about $12000000 USD!

Cryptocurrency backed by blockchain technology might be the new technological revolution in the modern world. It is time for people to gain some knowledge and insights on blockchain and cryptocurrency.

REFERENCES

1. https://www.coinmarket.com
2. https://live.blockcypher.com
3. https://www.blockchain.com
4. https://www.thebalance.com
5. https://www.coinatmradar.com
6. https://www.wikipedia.com

APPENDICES

Appendix I: Top 50 Cryptocurrency Exchanges
(www.coinmarket.com)

Binance

Coinbase Pro

Huobi Global

Kraken

Bitfinex

FTX

KuCoin

Upbit

Bitstamp

Poloniex

Bittrex

Coinone

Bithumb

Indodax

Gate.io

bitFlyer

Zaif

Liquid

BtcTurk | Pro

Luno

Binance.US

Bitso

Gemini

Paribu

Mercado Bitcoin

CoinEx

CEX.IO

Bithumb Global

WazirX

Korbit

eToroX

OKEx

HitBTC

OceanEx

Rekeningku.com

CoinDCX

YoBit

BitMax

Bitcoin.com Exchange

WhiteBIT

Coinbit

Huobi Korea

Bitrue

Coinsbit

Coineal

Huobi Russia

MXC (MoCha)

Hotbit

BKEX

Folgory

Appendix II: Top 100 Cryptocurrencies
([www.coinmarket.com]( ))

- Bitcoin
- Ethereum
- Tether
- XRP
- Bitcoin Cash
- Binance Coin
- Polkadot
- Chainlink
- Bitcoin SV
- Cardano
- Crypto.com Coin
- Litecoin
- USD Coin

EOS
TRON
Tezos
Monero
Stellar
Neo
UNUS SED LEO
NEM
Cosmos
Wrapped Bitcoin
Huobi Token
Dai
VeChain
yearn.finance
IOTA
Aave
THETA
Dash
Ethereum Classic
Zcash
OMG Network
UMA
Maker
TrueUSD
Synthetix Network Token
Ontology
Binance USD
Uniswap
HedgeTrade
OKB
Algorand
FTX Token
Basic Attention Token
Dogecoin

Compound
DigiByte
0x
BitTorrent
Kusama
Celo
Hyperion
Loopring
Energy Web Token
Waves
Paxos Standard
ICON
Qtum
Celsius
NXM
Kyber Network
ABBC Coin
Ren
Hedera Hashgraph
Arweave
Zilliqa
The Midas Touch Gold
Augur
SushiSwap
Lisk
ZB Token
Decred
Elrond
Bitcoin Gold
CyberVein
Band Protocol
Enjin Coin
Siacoin
Decentraland

Terra
HUSD
Ocean Protocol
DFI.Money
Revain
Aragon
Swipe
Solana
Quant
Nervos Network
Orchid
Nano
DxChain Token
Golem
Balancer
Bitcoin Diamond
Avalanche
Ravencoin
Bytom
Numeraire

Appendix III: Crypto ATMs Around the World
(www.coinatmradar.com)

United States

(8270 locations)

Canada

(896 locations)

United Kingdom

(281 locations)

Austria

(152 locations)

Spain

(109 locations)

Switzerland

(81 locations)

Poland

(66 locations)

Italy

(66 locations)

Czech Republic

(63 locations)

Hong Kong

(62 locations)

Colombia

(59 locations)

Greece

(55 locations)

Russian Federation

(53 locations)

Romania

(53 locations)

Slovakia

(49 locations)

Hungary

(47 locations)

Netherlands

(40 locations)

Belgium

(30 locations)

Germany

(29 locations)

Georgia

(26 locations)

Ukraine

(23 locations)

Ireland

(22 locations)

Australia

(19 locations)

Panama

(18 locations)

Dominican Republic

(16 locations)

Slovenia

(15 locations)

Argentina

(13 locations)

Bulgaria

(12 locations)

Taiwan

(12 locations)

France

(11 locations)

Finland

(10 locations)

Mexico

(10 locations)

Singapore

(9 locations)

South Africa

(9 locations)

Puerto Rico

(8 locations)

VietNam

(8 locations)

Estonia

(7 locations)

Thailand

(6 locations)

Serbia

(6 locations)

Israel

(6 locations)

Croatia

(5 locations)

Liechtenstein

(4 locations)

Philippines

(4 locations)

Kazakhstan

(3 locations)

Peru

(3 locations)

Portugal

(3 locations)

Chile

(3 locations)

Bahamas

(3 locations)

Kosovo

(3 locations)

Guam

(2 locations)

Ghana

(2 locations)

Lebanon

(2 locations)

Turkey

(2 locations)

Costa Rica

(2 locations)

Bahrain

(2 locations)

Uganda

(1 location)

United Arab Emirates

(1 location)

Venezuela

(1 location)

Anguilla

(1 location)

Saudi Arabia

(1 location)

San Marino

(1 location)

Saint Kitts and Nevis

(1 location)

Norway

(1 location)

Nigeria

(1 location)

Malaysia

(1 location)

Lithuania

(1 location)

Kenya

(1 location)

India

(1 location)

El Salvador

(1 location)

Ecuador

(1 location)

Djibouti

(1 location)

Botswana

(1 location)

Barbados

(1 location)

Aruba

(1 location)

Zimbabwe

(1 location)

www.ingramcontent.com/pod-product-compliance
Lightning Source LLC
Chambersburg PA
CBHW071306050326
40690CB00011B/2543